GREEN BOND MARKET SURVEY FOR THE LAO PEOPLE'S DEMOCRATIC REPUBLIC

INSIGHTS ON THE PERSPECTIVES OF INSTITUTIONAL INVESTORS AND UNDERWRITERS

SEPTEMBER 2022

ASIAN DEVELOPMENT BANK

ADB

© 2022 Asian Development Bank
6 ADB Avenue, Mandaluyong City, 1550 Metro Manila, Philippines
Tel +63 2 8632 4444; Fax +63 2 8636 2444
www.adb.org

Some rights reserved. Published in 2022.

ISBN 978-92-9269-725-9 (print); 978-92-9269-726-6 (electronic); 978-92-9269-727-3 (ebook)
Publication Stock No. TCS220369-2
DOI: http://dx.doi.org/10.22617/TCS220369-2

The views expressed in this publication are those of the authors and do not necessarily reflect the views and policies of the Asian Development Bank (ADB) or its Board of Governors or the governments they represent.

ADB does not guarantee the accuracy of the data included in this publication and accepts no responsibility for any consequence of their use. The mention of specific companies or products of manufacturers does not imply that they are endorsed or recommended by ADB in preference to others of a similar nature that are not mentioned.

By making any designation of or reference to a particular territory or geographic area, or by using the term "country" in this document, ADB does not intend to make any judgments as to the legal or other status of any territory or area.

Please contact pubsmarketing@adb.org if you have questions or comments with respect to content, or if you wish to obtain copyright permission for your intended use that does not fall within these terms, or for permission to use the ADB logo.

Corrigenda to ADB publications may be found at http://www.adb.org/publications/corrigenda.

Cover design by Mike Cortes.

CONTENTS

TABLE AND FIGURES

ACKNOWLEDGMENTS

The lead authors, Kosintr Puongsophol, financial sector specialist, Oth Marulou Gagni, senior operations assistant, and Alita Lestor, consultant, all from the Economic Research and Regional Cooperation Department (ERCD) of the Asian Development Bank, would like to particularly thank Satoru Yamadera, advisor, ERCD; Richard Supangan, senior economics officer, ERCD; Emma Allen, senior country economist, Lao People's Democratic Republic (Lao PDR) Resident Mission; and Soulinthone Leuangkhamsing, senior economics officer, Lao PDR Resident Mission for their support and contributions. Editing by Kevin Donahue. Design and layout by Prince Nicdao.

The lead authors would like to thank the ASEAN Secretariat and the Nomura Research Institute—its consultant under the ASEAN+3 Asian Bond Market Initiative's Technical Assistance Coordination Team led by Jonathan Panggabean, Kengo Mizuno, Pimpadcha Kerdkokaew, and Dollaporn Khositphumiveth—for their inputs. Furthermore, the lead authors wish to acknowledge support from the Global Green Growth Institute team comprising Srinath Komarina, Hien Tran, Thinh Tran, Minh Tran, and Ha Nguyen.

Finally, we would like to express our heartfelt gratitude to the local regulatory authorities, the Bank of the Lao PDR and the Lao Securities Commission Office, and all respondents in the Lao PDR for their assistance with and participation in the survey.

ABBREVIATIONS

ABMI	ASEAN+3 Asian Bond Markets Initiative
ADB	Asian Development Bank
ASEAN	Association of Southeast Asian Nations
ASEAN+3	ASEAN plus the People's Republic of China, Japan, and the Republic of Korea
ESG	environmental, social, and governance
LCY	local currency
LSCO	Lao Securities Commission Office
SDG	Sustainable Development Goal
USD	United States dollar

SUMMARY AND KEY FINDINGS

SURVEY HIGHLIGHTS

In December 2021, the Asian Development Bank and the Global Green Growth Institute conducted an online survey and received a total of nine responses from institutional investors and underwriters in the Lao People's Democratic Republic (Lao PDR). Given the size and current stage of capital market development in the Lao PDR, the number of responses provides us with a good indication of the interest of local market participants. The survey was conducted to assess institutional investors' interest in green bonds issued in the Lao PDR, as well as the perspectives of local underwriters on their clients' interest in green bond issuance. The survey identified the market drivers, impediments, and development priorities to assist development partners in identifying potential areas of support to accelerate the development of the Lao PDR's sustainable finance market. The most noteworthy survey findings are presented below:

▶ Almost 60% of institutional investors participating in the survey indicated that they are keen to explore possible investment opportunities in green bonds but lack the resources to do so. Similarly, approximately 80% of local underwriters have reported that their clients are interested in issuing green bonds but lack the necessary resources.

▶ The lack of policy guidance from regulators and the absence of internal resources were cited as the primary obstacles preventing local investors from investing in green bonds. From the perspective of underwriters, the lack of resources to launch new products in the Lao PDR was cited as a major obstacle.

▶ Both investors and underwriters agreed that the most promising sectors for growth in the Lao PDR's green bond market are sustainable agriculture and renewable energy.

▶ To attract investments, green bonds must provide a higher return than conventional bonds and allow investors to diversify their portfolios. Meanwhile, underwriters indicated that the opportunity to attract new investors would be the primary reason for issuing green bonds, followed by improved corporate disclosure and potentially lower funding costs.

▶ Development banks can play a number of roles in accelerating growth in the green bond market.

The Lao PDR's green bond market is still in its early stages of development. Nearly 60% of institutional investors are willing to explore the possibility of investing in green bonds but lack the resources to do so, while 30% of respondents are not interested at this time. Only 10% of respondents are currently developing an action plan. In addition, approximately 80% of underwriters stated that while they and their clients are willing to explore the possibility of green bond issuance, a lack of resources is the primary factor holding them back.

An absence of regulatory guidance and resources is impeding market development. The policy to develop a sustainable bond market in the Lao PDR was only introduced earlier this year under the Capital Market Development Strategy, 2021–2025. Program No. 4 of this strategy aims to expand and strengthen listed companies and develop securities products. While the Lao Securities Commission Office has been examining key characteristics and exploring a practical regulatory framework for sustainable bonds and corporate bonds in general, this has yet to be communicated to the market. In the meantime, the majority of investors and underwriters indicated that the lack of necessary resources is one of the primary obstacles for the Lao PDR to develop a green bond market, and that additional capacity building support from regulators and development partners is necessary.

Renewable energy and sustainable agriculture are the sectors with the highest growth potential. Survey respondents, both investors and underwriters, shared the view that renewable energy and sustainable agriculture are the two sectors with the most potential for green bond investment and issuance (**Table**).

Table: Sectors with Highest Growth Potential for Green Bond Investment and Issuance (%)

Investors			Underwriters		
Renewable Energy	Sustainable Agriculture	Clean Transportation	Sustainable Agriculture	Renewable Energy	Clean Transportation and Energy Efficiency
35	26	17	38	31	15

Source: Authors' compilation based on survey results.

Unlike underwriters, investors have a clear preference for smaller investment sizes. All investors who responded to the survey indicated a willingness to invest less than USD10 million per green bond transaction. In contrast, 40% of underwriters seek green bond issuance sizes between USD10 million and USD50 million, while 60% seek issuances of less than USD10 million per transaction.

The company profile is seen as the most critical factor for investing. Nearly 70% of respondents indicated that the profile of a company is their primary consideration when investing in green bonds. Other factors such as credit rating, historical performance, and valuation played a lesser role. Given that there is neither a corporate nor a sustainable bond market in the Lao PDR, key features of sustainable bonds such as environmental, social, and governance impacts and external review, were deemed among the least significant factors.

Tax incentives could be a key driver for market development. Investors and underwriters agreed that tax incentives could be a key factor in the development of a sustainable bond market. While this measure was viewed as a key driver, proper analysis must be made to ensure its effectiveness and to prevent any unexpected consequences on other aspects of the financial system. Underwriters also indicated that other factors—such as increased investor demand, the availability of local green bond verifiers and providers of second party opinions, and the existence of a green taxonomy—are equally important.

While investors are looking to get higher returns, underwriters are looking to broaden the investor base. All investors who participated in the survey agreed that green bonds should offer a higher rate of return than traditional bonds and allow investors to diversify their portfolios. However, underwriters indicated that the opportunity to attract new investors would be the primary reason for issuing green bonds, followed by enhanced corporate disclosure and the possibility of reduced funding costs.

INTRODUCTION

Background and Objective

The Asian Development Bank (ADB) is collaborating closely with the Association of Southeast Asian Nations (ASEAN), the People's Republic of China, Japan, and the Republic of Korea—collectively known as ASEAN+3—to promote the development of local currency (LCY) bond markets and regional bond market integration through the Asian Bond Markets Initiative (ABMI). ABMI was established in 2002 to bolster the resilience of ASEAN+3 financial systems by developing LCY bond markets as an alternative source to foreign-currency-denominated, short-term bank loans for long-term investment financing.

ADB, as Secretariat for the ABMI, is implementing a regional technical assistance (TA) program to promote sustainable LCY bond market development with support from the People's Republic of China's Poverty Reduction and Regional Cooperation Fund. This TA was developed and is being implemented with guidance from ASEAN+3 finance ministers and central bank governors, and in accordance with the ABMI Medium-Term Road Map for 2019–2022.

This survey report, conducted in collaboration with the Global Green Growth Institute, aims to assess institutional investors' interest in green bonds issued in the Lao People's Democratic Republic (Lao PDR), as well as the perspectives of local arrangers and underwriters on their clients' interest in green bond issuance. The survey aims to identify market drivers, impediments, and development priorities for the Lao PDR's sustainable finance market to assist development partners in identifying potential areas of support to accelerate the market's development.

Methodologies

In December 2021, ADB conducted the survey via an online platform, Microsoft Forms. A total of nine respondents participated in the survey. The respondents are engaged with investment banks (commercial banks and securities companies), a state-owned bank's treasury department, and a commercial bank's treasury department. The respondents hold various positions in their organization: the majority are middle management, while a respectable number are senior management or executive or C-level (i.e., CEO, CFO, CIO).

OVERVIEW OF THE LAO PEOPLE'S DEMOCRATIC REPUBLIC'S SUSTAINABLE BOND MARKET

The bond market of the Lao PDR is in the nascent stage of development. While there have been government bond issuances in the domestic market, LCY corporate bonds have been nonexistent since the first Regulation on Corporate Bond Issuance was promulgated in 2014. Nonetheless, three corporations have issued foreign currency-denominated bonds in offshore markets. Despite the fact that the use of proceeds of the government and some corporate issuers pertain to one or several dimensions of the 17 United Nations Sustainable Development Goals (SDGs) such as SDG 7 (Affordable and Clean Energy), SDG 8 (Decent Work and Economic Growth), and SDG 9 (Industry, Innovation, and Infrastructure) with indirect potential consequences on poverty relief, none of these bonds are issued under the sustainable bond framework.[1] In fact, it is difficult, if not impossible, to determine the extent to which these bonds comply with the sustainable bond standards since there is no reporting system based on corporate social responsibility or environmental, social, and governance (ESG) standards in the Lao PDR at the moment.

Corporate bond issuance is provided for by the Law on Securities and implemented through the Regulation on Corporate Bond Issuance, which specifies conditions and procedures regarding corporate bond activities. Other relevant regulations include the Regulation on Bondholder Representatives and the Regulation on Bond Listing. In 2021, the Regulation on Issuance of Corporate Bonds, first promulgated in 2014, was amended to ease several provisions regarding preconditions for an issuer's financial stance and a requirement of supporting documents for issuance application.

Government bond issuance is regulated under the Law on State Budget and Law on Public Debt Management, and it is primarily implemented through the Decree on Government Bonds. The latter prescribes type, issuance approach, offering, issuance, redemption, reporting procedure, and eligible investors in government bonds.

None of these laws or regulations have yet given attention to sustainable finance within the capital market, but rather they have focused on laying down the fundamental conditions necessary for the initial stage of market development.

---

[1] United Nations Capital Development Fund. 2021. *SDG Financing in Lao PDR: A Synthesis Report*. New York.

RECENT INITIATIVES ON SUSTAINABLE FINANCE

Sustainable socioeconomic development has been one of the priorities of the Lao PDR as indicated by the 5-year National Socioeconomic Development Plan and the National Green Growth Strategy, 2030. However, the banking sector is at the initial stage of making a commitment to the Sustainable Banking Network to integrate ESG risk management in business operation and increase capital flows to activities with positive climate impact.[2] Meanwhile, a path toward development of sustainable finance in the capital market was introduced by the Lao Securities Commission Office (LSCO) in early 2022 under the Capital Market Development Strategy, 2021–2025. As such, the concepts of sustainable finance—including a green definition or taxonomy, sustainability risk management, sustainability disclosure, and a sustainability index—are new to both regulators as well as market participants in the Lao PDR, thus the ongoing initiatives raise awareness and build capacity for all relevant stakeholders.

National Green Growth Strategy

Moving toward becoming an upper middle-income country in accordance with green and sustainable growth and achieving the SDGs by 2030, the Government of the Lao PDR appointed the National Steering Committee for Green Growth with the deputy prime minister and the minister of finance as co-chairs. The committee launched the National Green Growth Strategy in 2018 as a supplement to the National Socioeconomic Development Plan, with a vision to 2030 to ensure that green and sustainable direction are integrated into development efforts for every sector.

Under the National Green Growth Strategy, the banking sectors is considered a supporting sector to promote sustainable development through monetary policy such as low-interest rate loans for investment in sectors related to green and sustainable development. However, there is no regulation or provision for the inclusion of such initiatives in the monetary policies and practices of the banking sector in the Lao PDR yet.

Capital Market Development Strategy

As mentioned above, the LSCO launched the Capital Market Development Strategy, 2021–2025 which comprises five programs relevant to debt securities:

(i)   strengthen the LSCO;
(ii) develop and amend legislation and policy;

---

[2] International Finance Corporation. 2019. *Global Progress Report of the Sustainable Banking Network Innovations in Policy and Industry Actions in Emerging Markets*. Washington, DC.

(iii) strengthen capital market infrastructure;
(iv) expand and strengthen listed companies and develop securities products; and
(v) expand, protect, and strengthen investors and market participants.

Sustainable bonds are one of the new securities products aimed to be developed under Program No. 4 of the Capital Market Development Strategy, 2021–2025. The LSCO is studying implementation mechanisms and needed legislation in the context of issuing green, social, and sustainability bonds in the domestic market to support sustainable finance and socioeconomic development in the Lao PDR. In this regard, a workshop on sustainability bonds was organized under the Asian Bond Markets Initiative in March 2022 to raise awareness among stakeholders of the regulatory framework and international standards and practices. Workshop attendees included the relevant regulators and market participants such as securities firms and listed companies.

To support the sustainable bond market's development in the Lao PDR, the LSCO aims to develop a standardized prospectus and adopt the Single Submission Form for bond issuance under the ASEAN+3 Multi-Currency Bond Issuance Framework. Additionally, local companies will be encouraged to implement corporate governance practices and adopt International Financial Reporting Standards in business reporting to promote the confidence of domestic and foreign investors in both domestic and offshore issuance.

SURVEY RESULTS

The survey was conducted in December 2021 among local institutional investors, including fund managers, financial institutions, insurance companies, and local underwriters and advisors. A summary of the survey's findings is given below.

Institutional Investors

The survey began by asking respondents about firms' interest and/or current investments in green financial instruments. More than 50% of firms that responded are exploring possible investment opportunities but with limited awareness and resources, while 30% indicated that they are not interested at this stage. Only a small number of responses indicated that they are already developing an action plan (**Figure 1**).

When asked about issuance size, all respondents indicated a preference for transactions involving less than USD10 million. This is consistent with the Lao PDR's early stage of bond market development (**Figure 2**).

When asked about key motivations for investing in green bonds, the majority of respondents believe that having an improved green image in their institution's investment strategy is critical. Meanwhile, institutional investors believed that investing in green bonds would help them diversify their portfolios and generate excess returns. Additionally, the increased transparency of their investment portfolios would be a significant factor in deciding whether to invest in green bonds (**Figure 3**). While all respondents stated that one of their primary motivations is

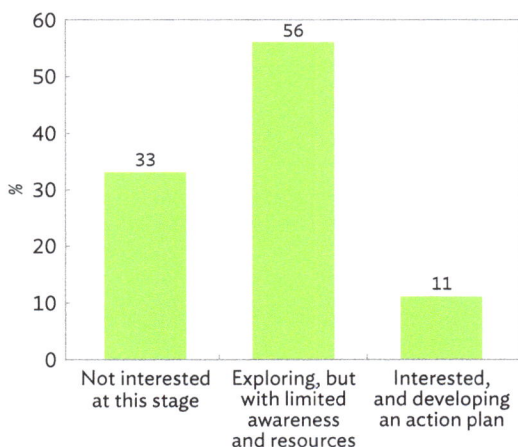

Figure 1: Interest in Investing in Green Bonds

Source: Authors' compilation based on survey results.

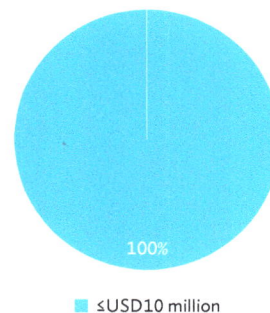

Figure 2: Optimal Investment Size

USD = United States dollar.
Source: Authors' compilation based on survey results.

Figure 3: Key Motivations for Investing in Green Bonds

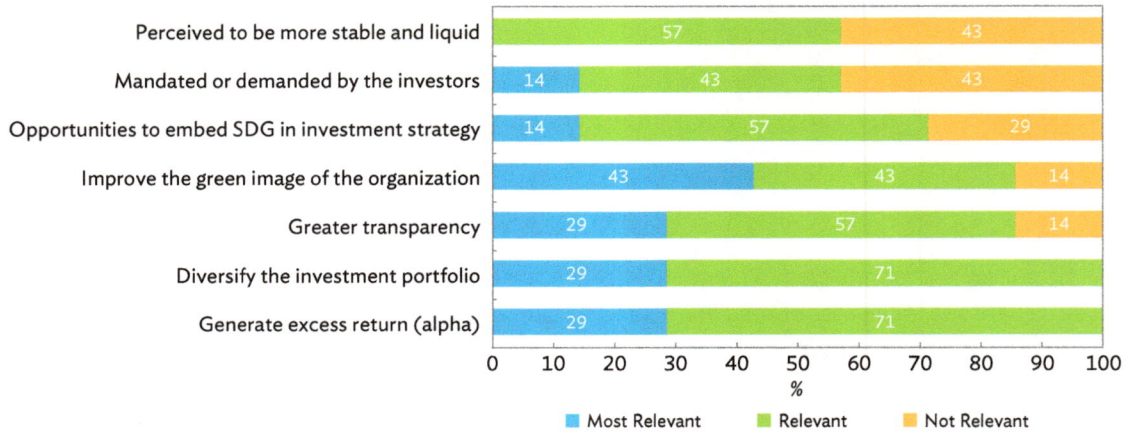

Motivation	Most Relevant	Relevant	Not Relevant
Perceived to be more stable and liquid		57	43
Mandated or demanded by the investors	14	43	43
Opportunities to embed SDG in investment strategy	14	57	29
Improve the green image of the organization	43	43	14
Greater transparency	29	57	14
Diversify the investment portfolio	29	71	
Generate excess return (alpha)	29	71	

SDG = Sustainable Development Goal.
Source: Authors' compilation based on survey results.

to generate excess return, it is critical to keep in mind that this may not be possible given the Lao PDR's bond market's infancy.

To help local regulators develop the green bond market, investors were asked to identify any major obstacles to investing in green bonds. The majority of respondents indicated that the primary impediments are the absence of policy guidance from regulators related to green bonds, as well as the lack of internal resources for such investments. Meanwhile, more than 20% of respondents felt that there is a lack of clear benefits for investing in green bonds as opposed to conventional bonds, while a small number of respondents indicated that having limited funds is one of the major impediments (**Figure 4**).

Figure 4: Main Obstacles to Investing in Green Bonds

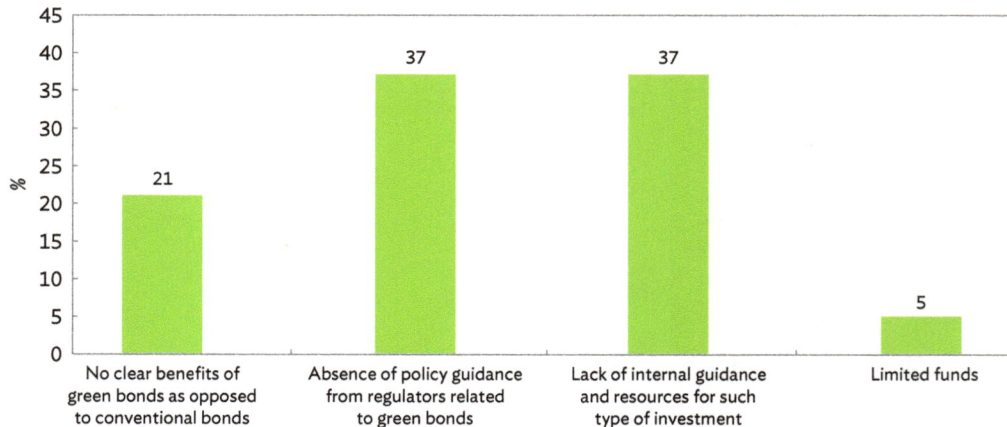

Obstacle	%
No clear benefits of green bonds as opposed to conventional bonds	21
Absence of policy guidance from regulators related to green bonds	37
Lack of internal guidance and resources for such type of investment	37
Limited funds	5

Source: Authors' compilation based on survey results.

Respondents shared that if they are to invest in green bonds, they will place emphasis on the company's profile and management team, as well as the bond's valuation and pricing. Credit rating is also critical from an investor's perspective, particularly if green bonds are to be issued by corporate issuers. While the majority of investors believe that the external review of green bonds is necessary, only a small percentage believe that it is a critical factor for investing in green bonds (**Figure 5**).

Respondents were asked to choose up to three options that they believe could help the growth of the Lao PDR's green bond market. Almost 25% of responses suggested that tax incentives and subsidies for green bond issuers and investors would be a critical driver of sustainable bond market development. Meanwhile, nearly 20% of respondents said that both increased stakeholder demand and the promotion of ESG reporting on the securities exchange would significantly help investors to make green investment decisions. Respondents also thought that an independent review of green bonds

was important, albeit to a lesser extent than increased demand and promoting ESG investing. This finding is consistent with a previous question about the most important factors to consider when investing in green bonds, in which investors indicated that the external review of green bonds is less important (**Figure 6**).

Local institutional investors indicated that they are most interested in green bonds issued by the government, followed by those issued by financial institutions and development banks (**Figure 7**).

As for nonfinancial institutions, the survey further investigated which industries present the greatest potential for green bond investments. Nearly 40% of respondents indicated that renewable energy and sustainable agriculture are the most promising sectors for the Lao PDR to develop its domestic sustainable bond market. Several respondents also expressed an interest in the clean transportation and energy efficiency sectors (**Figure 8**).

Figure 5: Key Considerations for Investing in Green Bonds

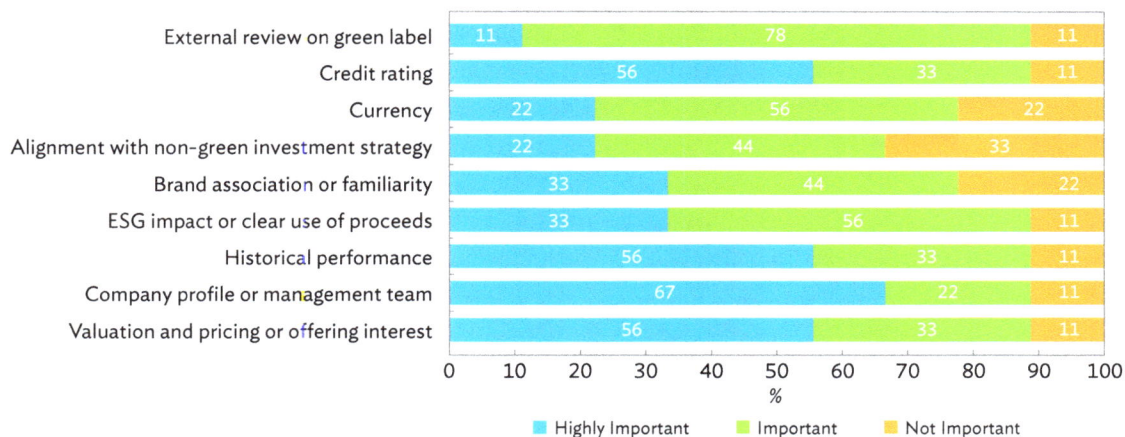

ESG = environmental, social, and governance.
Source: Authors' compilation based on survey results.

Figure 6: Policy Mechanisms That Would Increase Green Bond Investments

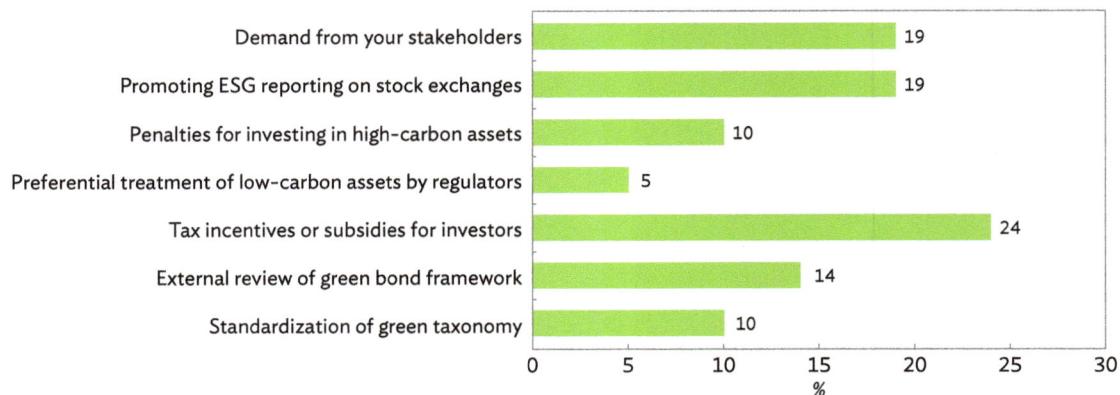

	%
Demand from your stakeholders	19
Promoting ESG reporting on stock exchanges	19
Penalties for investing in high-carbon assets	10
Preferential treatment of low-carbon assets by regulators	5
Tax incentives or subsidies for investors	24
External review of green bond framework	14
Standardization of green taxonomy	10

ESG = environmental, social, and governance.
Source: Authors' compilation based on survey results.

Figure 7: Types of Issuers That Local Investors Most Want to Invest In

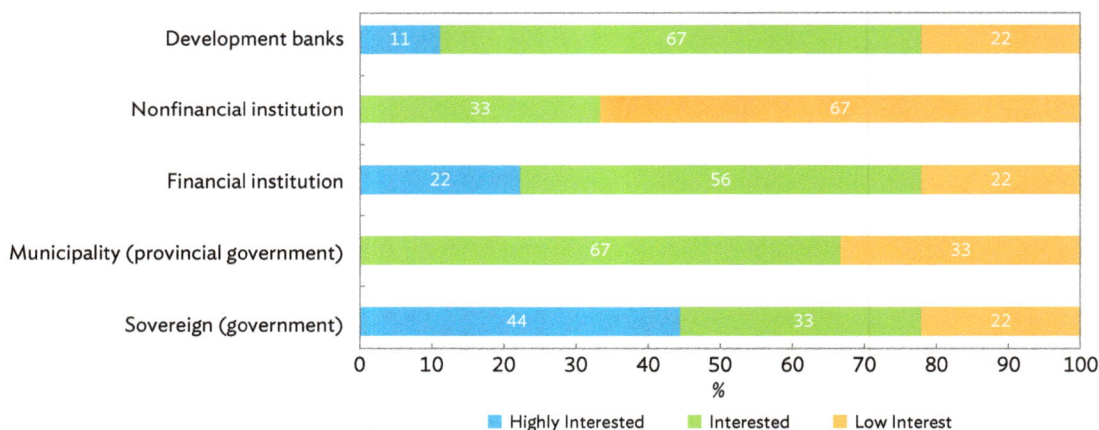

	Highly Interested	Interested	Low Interest
Development banks	11	67	22
Nonfinancial institution		33	67
Financial institution	22	56	22
Municipality (provincial government)		67	33
Sovereign (government)	44	33	22

Source: Authors' compilation based on survey results.

Given the lack of green bond issuance in the Lao PDR, respondents were asked whether they would be interested to invest in other member economies of the Association of Southeast Asian Nations. A majority of local institutional investors indicated they currently have no intention of investing in green bonds issued in other countries. However, among those expressing an interest, Viet Nam, followed by Singapore and Thailand, are their preferred investment destinations (**Figure 9**). When asked about the underlying currency, over 93% of respondents prefer the United States dollar, euro, or Thai baht (**Figure 10**).

Figure 8: Sectors with Most Potential for Green Bond Investments

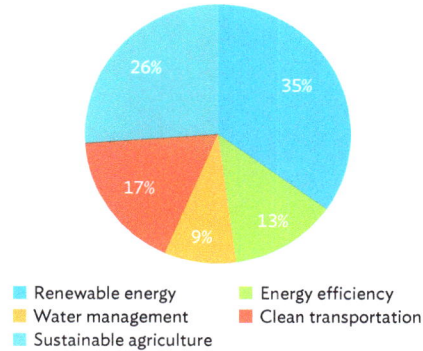

- Renewable energy 35%
- Sustainable agriculture 26%
- Clean transportation 17%
- Energy efficiency 13%
- Water management 9%

Source: Authors' compilation based on survey results.

Figure 9: Interest in Regional Investment

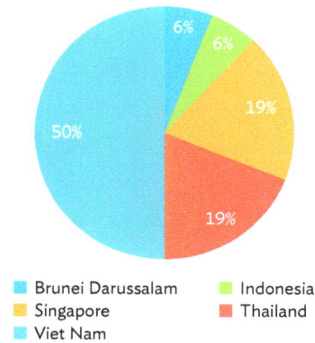

- Brunei Darussalam 50%
- Singapore 19%
- Thailand 19%
- Indonesia 6%
- Viet Nam 6%

Source: Authors' compilation based on survey results.

All respondents emphasized the critical importance of government and regulatory policy clarity for the Lao PDR to develop a domestic green bond market. Indeed, nearly 80% of respondents considered this to be the most critical factor. Additionally, respondents believed that tax incentives and subsidies for green bond issuers and investors, as well as the presence of a centralized information platform for the country's sustainable bond market, would significantly aid them in making green investment decisions (**Figure 11**).

Regarding capacity development, respondents agreed that deal teams inside investment banks and securities firms require additional training. This would also enable them to provide advisory services to their clients who wish to issue a green bond. Additionally, investors, chief financial officers of listed companies, and board members of state-owned banks and enterprises should be trained to gain a better understanding of green bonds and encouraged to increase the supply of green bonds to meet investor demand (**Figure 12**).

Figure 10: Preferred Underlying Investment Currencies

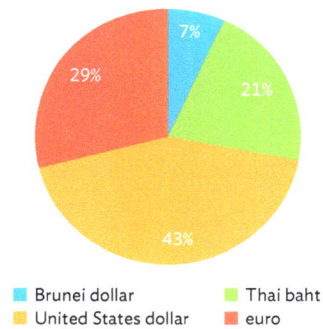

- United States dollar 43%
- euro 29%
- Thai baht 21%
- Brunei dollar 7%

Source: Authors' compilation based on survey results.

Figure 11: Policy Options for Green Bond Market Development

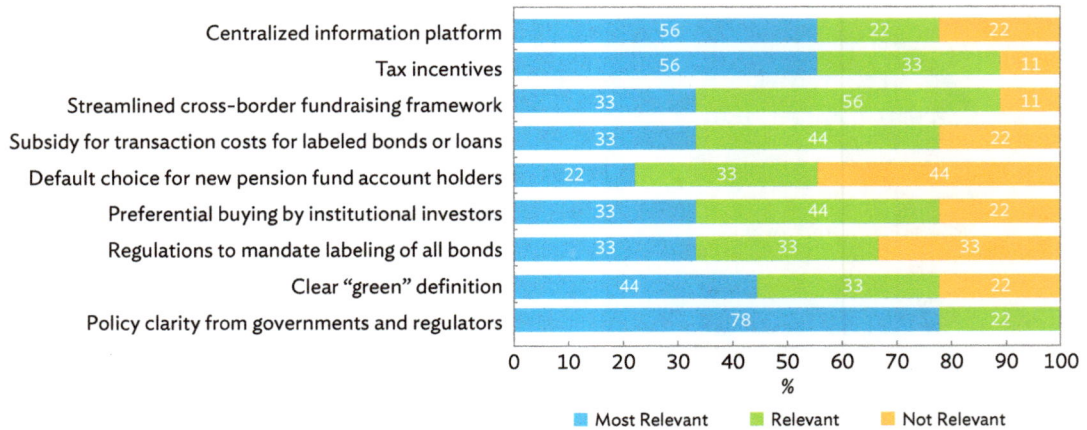

Policy Option	Most Relevant	Relevant	Not Relevant
Centralized information platform	56	22	22
Tax incentives	56	33	11
Streamlined cross-border fundraising framework	33	56	11
Subsidy for transaction costs for labeled bonds or loans	33	44	22
Default choice for new pension fund account holders	22	33	44
Preferential buying by institutional investors	33	44	22
Regulations to mandate labeling of all bonds	33	33	33
Clear "green" definition	44	33	22
Policy clarity from governments and regulators	78	22	

Source: Authors' compilation based on survey results.

Figure 12: Capacity Building—Who Should Be Trained?

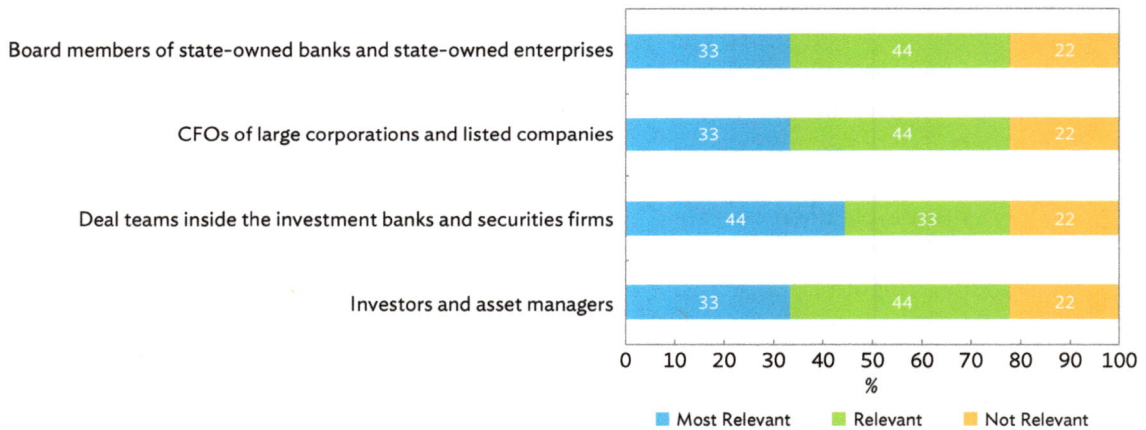

	Most Relevant	Relevant	Not Relevant
Board members of state-owned banks and state-owned enterprises	33	44	22
CFOs of large corporations and listed companies	33	44	22
Deal teams inside the investment banks and securities firms	44	33	22
Investors and asset managers	33	44	22

CFO = chief financial officer.
Source: Authors' compilation based on survey results.

Advisors and Underwriters

Based on responses from local advisors and underwriters, this section examines the potential of green bond issuance, promising economic sectors, practical policy mechanisms, and the various types of potential issuers. Due to the small number of responses, this section may not reflect the market as a whole.

On the interest of green bond issuance, the majority of the respondents' clients are exploring, but with limited awareness and resources. This may be an area where development partners such as ADB can assist interested entities with technical assistance and capacity building. It was encouraging to learn that none of the respondents indicated their clients are opposed to green bond issuance (**Figure 13**).

Figure 13: Issuers' Interest in Issuing Green Bonds

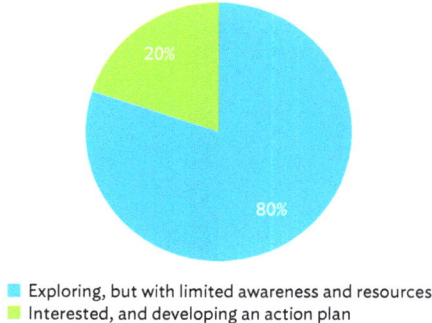

- Exploring, but with limited awareness and resources
- Interested, and developing an action plan

Source: Authors' compilation based on survey results.

Figure 14: Optimal Issuance Size

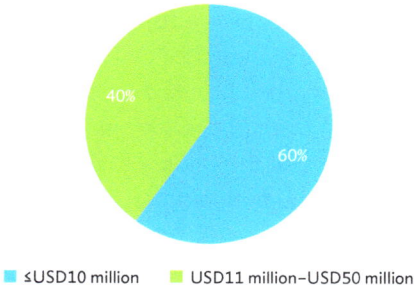

- ≤USD10 million
- USD11 million–USD50 million

USD = United States dollar.
Source: Authors' compilation based on survey results.

The optimal issuance size for green financial instruments in the respondents' market is not more than USD10 million. This is aligned with investors' response that they are looking for a ticket size of less than USD10 million per transaction (**Figure 14**).

When asked why clients want to issue green bonds, approximately 80% indicated that green bonds could help issuers attract new investors. Additionally, all respondents believed that green bond issuance would enable issuers to enhance the quality of corporate disclosures. Moreover, respondents agreed that issuing green bonds would enable issuers to lower their cost of capital and integrate an ESG approach into their corporate DNA, thereby improving the organization's green image (**Figure 15**).

Figure 15: Key Motivations for Issuing Green Bonds

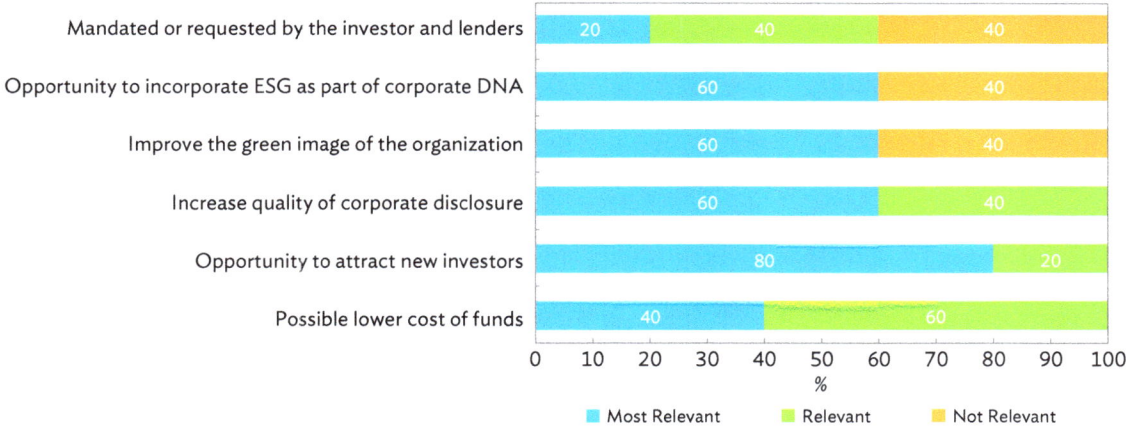

ESG = environmental, social, and governance.
Source: Authors' compilation based on survey results.

However, more than 40% of respondents cited a lack of internal guidance and resources to consider new products as a significant barrier to their clients issuing green bonds. The absence of clear benefits of green bonds over conventional bonds and the absence of policy guidance from regulators regarding the issuance of green bonds were also seen as significant barriers (**Figure 16**).

To overcome these obstacles, respondents were asked to identify policy mechanisms that would increase green bond issuance in the Lao PDR. The majority of respondents indicated that the primary factor to consider should be increased investor demand, as well as incentives or subsidies for green bond issuers and investors. Additionally, standardizing green taxonomies would provide clarity for green projects, as well as the development of local reviewers who communicate in the same language and understand market development (**Figure 17**).

In terms of sectors, all respondents agreed that sustainable agriculture presents the greatest opportunity for local issuers to issue green bonds over the next 3 years. This finding slightly contrasts with institutional investors'

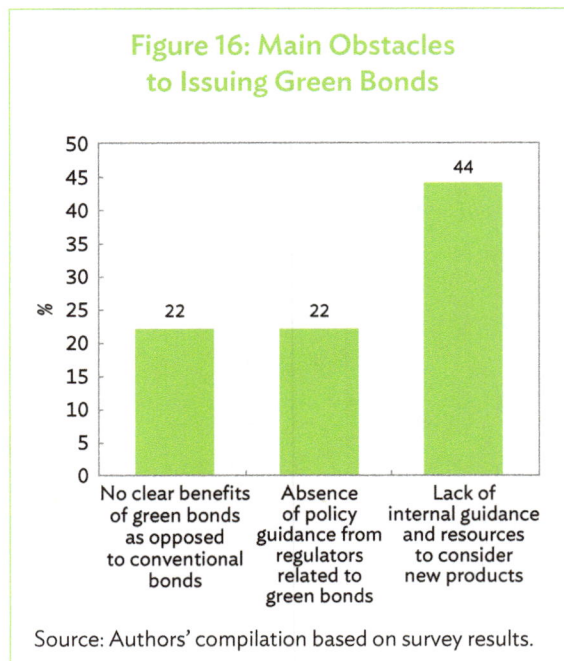

Figure 16: Main Obstacles to Issuing Green Bonds

Source: Authors' compilation based on survey results.

perspective, where sustainable agriculture ranked second to renewable energy. Additionally, over 60% of respondents agreed that the renewable energy, energy efficiency, and clean transportation sectors offer significant potential for the country's green bond market development (**Figure 18**).

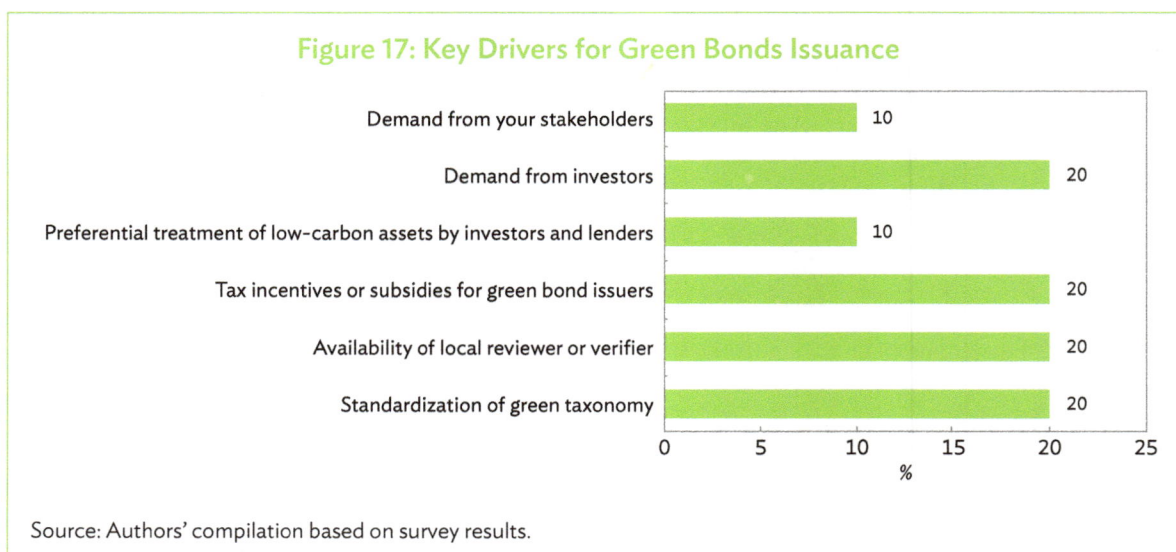

Figure 17: Key Drivers for Green Bonds Issuance

Source: Authors' compilation based on survey results.

Figure 18: Most Promising Sectors for Green Bonds Issuance

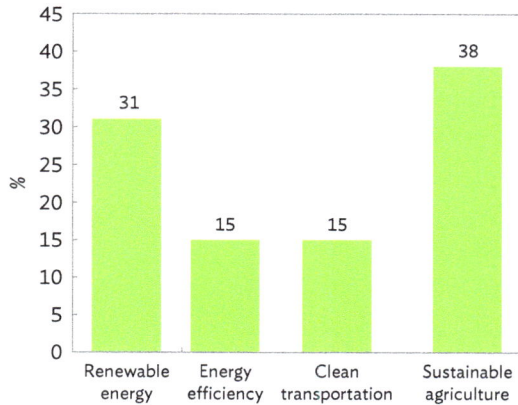

Source: Authors' compilation based on survey results.

with alternative investment opportunities (**Figure 19**).

To further develop the Lao PDR's green bond market, underwriters and advisors believe that policy clarity from government and regulators, as well as tax incentives for issuers and investors, are the most critical factors. Additionally, underwriters and advisors believed that making green and/or sustainability investments the default option for new pension fund account holders would increase demand for ESG products, including green bonds. Likewise, all respondents believed that external review and labeling a green bond would assist issuers in attracting new investors. This finding contrasts slightly with the perceptions of institutional investors, as only 14% of respondents believed this would increase investments in green bonds (**Figure 20**).

When asked about potential investors, all respondents indicated that commercial banks would be the primary investors of green bonds issued by their clients. Notably, all respondents agreed that having a mutual fund industry in the Lao PDR would be a critical driver of capital market development, particularly in the bond market. This would allow retail investors to invest in the bond market and provide local investors

In terms of currency, around 80% of respondents indicated that their clients would prefer to issue green bonds in local currency, while only 20% preferred to issue using hard currencies in international markets (**Figure 21**). For those interested in issuing green bond in foreign

Figure 19: Preferred Investors in Green Bonds

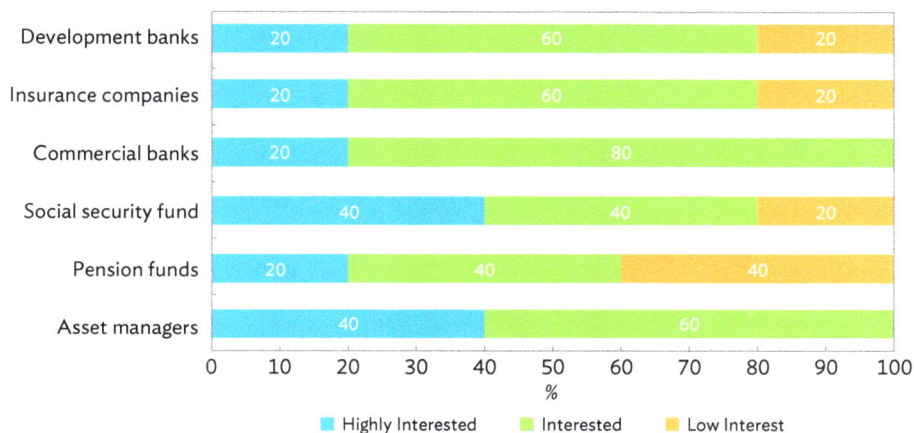

Source: Authors' compilation based on survey results.

Figure 20: Policy Options for Green Bond Market Development

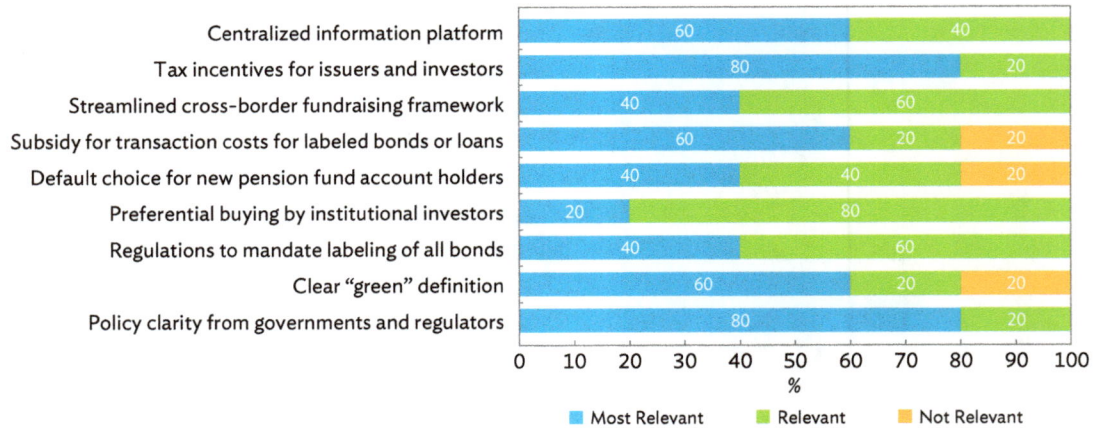

Policy Option	Most Relevant	Relevant	Not Relevant
Centralized information platform	60	40	
Tax incentives for issuers and investors	80	20	
Streamlined cross-border fundraising framework	40	60	
Subsidy for transaction costs for labeled bonds or loans	60	20	20
Default choice for new pension fund account holders	40	40	20
Preferential buying by institutional investors	20	80	
Regulations to mandate labeling of all bonds	40	60	
Clear "green" definition	60	20	20
Policy clarity from governments and regulators	80	20	

Source: Authors' compilation based on survey results.

Figure 21: Preferred Underlying Issuance Currencies

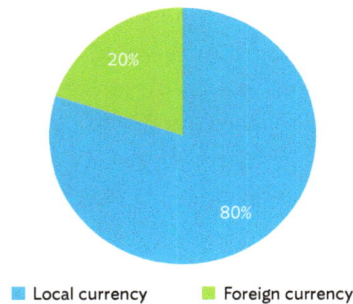

- Local currency: 80%
- Foreign currency: 20%

Source: Authors' compilation based on survey results.

Figure 22: Preferred Underlying Foreign Currencies

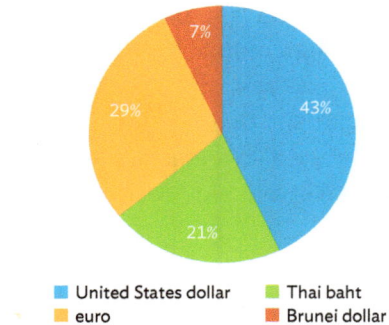

- United States dollar: 43%
- Thai baht: 21%
- euro: 29%
- Brunei dollar: 7%

Source: Authors' compilation based on survey results.

currencies, over 72% of respondents prefer hard currencies such as the United States dollar or euro (**Figure 22**).

In terms of capacity building, respondents suggested that all relevant stakeholders be trained (**Figure 23**). This could be an opportunity for development partners such as

ADB to raise awareness among local capital market stakeholders about the critical nature of climate change and how the capital market can help fund their efforts to address the issue. It is critical for all stakeholders, particularly state-owned enterprises and corporations, to understand that their operations can also help address climate issues.

Figure 23: Capacity Building—Who Should Be Trained?

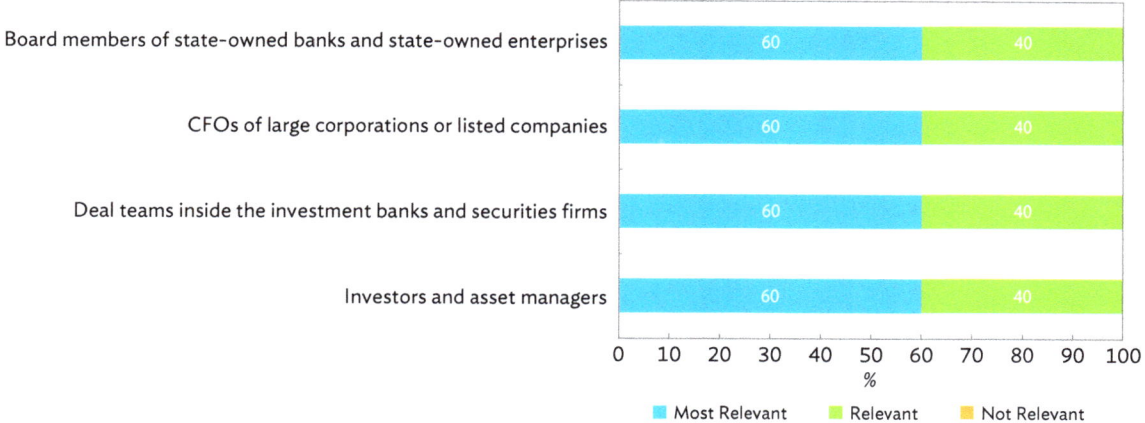

Board members of state-owned banks and state-owned enterprises	60 / 40
CFOs of large corporations or listed companies	60 / 40
Deal teams inside the investment banks and securities firms	60 / 40
Investors and asset managers	60 / 40

0 10 20 30 40 50 60 70 80 90 100
%

■ Most Relevant   ■ Relevant   ■ Not Relevant

CFO = chief financial officer.
Source: Authors' compilation based on survey results.

NEXT STEPS

The survey found that the majority of respondents are committed to environmental stewardship, whether as investors or underwriters. However, additional efforts are necessary, most notably in terms of capacity building for relevant stakeholders. Promoting a sustainable bond market alongside the development of the corporate bond market would be an ideal option for the Lao PDR. Simultaneously, it is critical to grow the domestic institutional investor base and streamline the bond issuance process for institutional investors.

It is important for the Lao PDR to have the first green bond issued in the country. A so-called "market champion" would increase awareness among local issuers and investors, and act as a catalyst for the development of the corporate bond market.

As Secretariat of the Asian Bond Markets Initiative, ADB will continue to collaborate closely with local regulatory bodies to establish and strengthen the ecosystem necessary for the development of the Lao PDR's sustainable finance market, including capacity building and technical assistance for issuers embarking on their sustainable finance journey.

www.ingramcontent.com/pod-product-compliance
Lightning Source LLC
Chambersburg PA
CBHW050058220326
41599CB00045B/7464